THE JPS B'NAI MITZVAH TORAH COMMENTARY

Va-yera' (Genesis 18:1–22:24)
Haftarah (2 Kings 4:1–37)

Rabbi Jeffrey K. Salkin

The Jewish Publication Society · Philadelphia
University of Nebraska Press · Lincoln

INTRODUCTION

News flash: the most important thing about becoming bar or bat mitzvah isn't the party. Nor is it the presents. Nor even being able to celebrate with your family and friends—as wonderful as those things are. Nor is it even standing before the congregation and reading the prayers of the liturgy—as important as that is.

No, the most important thing about becoming bar or bat mitzvah is sharing Torah with the congregation. And why is that? Because of all Jewish skills, that is the most important one.

Here is what is true about rites of passage: you can tell what a culture values by the tasks it asks its young people to perform on their way to maturity. In American culture, you become responsible for driving, responsible for voting, and yes, responsible for drinking responsibly.

In some cultures, the rite of passage toward maturity includes some kind of trial, or a test of strength. Sometimes, it is a kind of "outward bound" camping adventure. Among the Maasai tribe in Africa, it is traditional for a young person to hunt and kill a lion. In some Hispanic cultures, fifteen year-old girls celebrate the *quinceañera*, which marks their entrance into maturity.

What is Judaism's way of marking maturity? It combines both of these rites of passage: *responsibility* and *test*. You show that you are on your way to becoming a *responsible* Jewish adult through a public *test* of strength and knowledge—reading or chanting Torah, and then teaching it to the congregation.

This is the most important Jewish ritual mitzvah (commandment), and that is how you demonstrate that you are, truly, bar or bat mitzvah—old enough to be responsible for the mitzvot.

What Is Torah?

So, what exactly is the Torah? You probably know this already, but let's review.

The Torah (teaching) consists of "the five books of Moses," sometimes also called the *chumash* (from the Hebrew word *chameish*, which means "five"), or, sometimes, the Greek word Pentateuch (which means "the five teachings").

Here are the five books of the Torah, with their common names and their Hebrew names.

> **Genesis (The beginning), which in Hebrew is Bere'shit (from the first words—"When God began to create").** Bere'shit spans the years from Creation to Joseph's death in Egypt. Many of the Bible's best stories are in Genesis: the creation story itself; Adam and Eve in the Garden of Eden; Cain and Abel; Noah and the Flood; and the tales of the Patriarchs and Matriarchs, Abraham, Isaac, Jacob, Sarah, Rebekah, Rachel, and Leah. It also includes one of the greatest pieces of world literature, the story of Joseph, which is actually the oldest complete novel in history, comprising more than one-quarter of all Genesis.

> **Exodus (Getting out), which in Hebrew is Shemot (These are the names).** Exodus begins with the story of the Israelite slavery in Egypt. It then moves to the rise of Moses as a leader, and the Israelites' liberation from slavery. After the Israelites leave Egypt, they experience the miracle of the parting of the Sea of Reeds (or "Red Sea"); the giving of the Ten Commandments at Mount Sinai; the idolatry of the Golden Calf; and the design and construction of the Tabernacle and of the ark for the original tablets of the law, which our ancestors carried with them in the desert. Exodus also includes various ethical and civil laws, such as "You shall not wrong a stranger or oppress him, for you were strangers in the land of Egypt" (22:20).

> **Leviticus (about the Levites), or, in Hebrew, Va-yikra' (And God called).** It goes into great detail about the kinds of sacrifices that the ancient Israelites brought as offerings; the laws of ritual purity; the animals that were permitted and forbidden for eating (the beginnings of the tradition of kashrut, the Jewish dietary laws); the diagnosis of various skin diseases; the ethical laws of holiness; the ritual calendar of the Jewish year; and various agricultural laws concerning the treatment of the Land of Israel. Leviticus is basically the manual of ancient Judaism.

> Numbers (because the book begins with the census of the Isra-
elites), or, in Hebrew, Be-midbar (In the wilderness). The book
describes the forty years of wandering in the wilderness and the
various rebellions against Moses. The constant theme: "Egypt
wasn't so bad. Maybe we should go back." The greatest rebellion
against Moses was the negative reports of the spies about the
Land of Israel, which discouraged the Israelites from wanting to
move forward into the land. For that reason, the "wilderness generation" must die off before a new generation can come into maturity and finish the journey.

> Deuteronomy (The repetition of the laws of the Torah), or, in
Hebrew, Devarim (The words). The final book of the Torah is,
essentially, Moses's farewell address to the Israelites as they pre-
pare to enter the Land of Israel. Here we find various laws that
had been previously taught, though sometimes with different
wording. Much of Deuteronomy contains laws that will be important to the Israelites as they enter the Land of Israel—laws
concerning the establishment of a monarchy and the ethics of
warfare. Perhaps the most famous passage from Deuteronomy
contains the *Shema,* the declaration of God's unity and unique-
ness, and the *Ve-ahavta,* which follows it. Deuteronomy ends with
the death of Moses on Mount Nebo as he looks across the Jordan
Valley into the land that he will not enter.

Jews read the Torah in sequence—starting with Bere'shit right after Simchat Torah in the autumn, and then finishing Devarim on the
following Simchat Torah. Each Torah portion is called a parashah (di-
vision; sometimes called a *sidrah,* a place in the order of the Torah
reading). The stories go around in a full circle, reminding us that we
can always gain more insights and more wisdom from the Torah. This
means that if you don't "get" the meaning this year, don't worry—it
will come around again.

And What Else? The Haftarah

We read or chant the Torah from the Torah scroll—the most sacred
thing that a Jewish community has in its possession. The Torah is

written without vowels, and the ability to read it and chant it is part of the challenge and the test.

But there is more to the synagogue reading. Every Torah reading has an accompanying haftarah reading. Haftarah means "conclusion," because there was once a time when the service actually ended with that reading. Some scholars believe that the reading of the haftarah originated at a time when non-Jewish authorities outlawed the reading of the Torah, and the Jews read the haftarah sections instead. In fact, in some synagogues, young people who become bar or bat mitzvah read very little Torah and instead read the entire haftarah portion.

The haftarah portion comes from the Nevi'im, the prophetic books, which are the second part of the Jewish Bible. It is either read or chanted from a Hebrew Bible, or maybe from a booklet or a photocopy.

The ancient sages chose the haftarah passages because their themes reminded them of the words or stories in the Torah text. Sometimes, they chose *haftarah* with special themes in honor of a festival or an upcoming festival.

Not all books in the prophetic section of the Hebrew Bible consist of prophecy. Several are historical. For example:

The book of Joshua tells the story of the conquest and settlement of Israel.

The book of Judges speaks of the period of early tribal rulers who would rise to power, usually for the purpose of uniting the tribes in war against their enemies. Some of these leaders are famous: Deborah, the great prophetess and military leader, and Samson, the biblical strong man.

The books of Samuel start with Samuel, the last judge, and then move to the creation of the Israelite monarchy under Saul and David (approximately 1000 BCE).

The books of Kings tell of the death of King David, the rise of King Solomon, and how the Israelite kingdom split into the Northern Kingdom of Israel and the Southern Kingdom of Judah (approximately 900 BCE).

And then there are the books of the prophets, those spokesmen for God whose words fired the Jewish conscience. Their names are immortal: Isaiah, Jeremiah, Ezekiel, Amos, Hosea, among others.

Someone once said: "There is no evidence of a biblical prophet ever being invited back a second time for dinner." Why? Because the prophets were tough. They had no patience for injustice, apathy, or hypocrisy. No one escaped their criticisms. Here's what they taught:

> God commands the Jews to behave decently toward one another. In fact, God cares more about basic ethics and decency than about ritual behavior.
> God chose the Jews *not* for special privileges, but for special duties to humanity.
> As bad as the Jews sometimes were, there was always the possibility that they would improve their behavior.
> As bad as things might be now, it will not always be that way. Someday, there will be universal justice and peace. Human history is moving forward toward an ultimate conclusion that some call the Messianic Age: a time of universal peace and prosperity for the Jewish people and for all the people of the world.

Your Mission—To Teach Torah to the Congregation

On the day when you become bar or bat mitzvah, you will be reading, or chanting, Torah—in Hebrew. You will be reading, or chanting, the haftarah—in Hebrew. That is the major skill that publicly marks the becoming of bar or bat mitzvah. But, perhaps even more important than that, you need to be able to teach something about the Torah portion, and perhaps the haftarah as well.

And that is where this book comes in. It will be a very valuable resource for you, and your family, in the b'nai mitzvah process.

Here is what you will find in it:

> A brief **summary** of every Torah portion. This is a basic overview of the portion; and, while it might not refer to everything in the Torah portion, it will explain its most important aspects.
> A list of the **major ideas** in the Torah portion. The purpose: to make the Torah portion real, in ways that we can relate to. Every Torah portion contains unique ideas, and when you put all

of those ideas together, you actually come up with a list of Judaism's most important ideas.

> Two *divrei Torah* ("words of Torah," or "sermonettes") for each portion. These *divrei Torah* explain significant aspects of the Torah portion in accessible, reader-friendly language. Each *devar Torah* contains references to **traditional** Jewish sources (those that were written before the modern era), as well as **modern** sources and quotes. We have searched, far and wide, to find sources that are unusual, interesting, and not just the "same old stuff" that many people already know about the Torah portion. Why did we include these minisermons in the volume? Not because we want you to simply copy those sermons and pass them off as your own (that would be cheating), though you are free to quote from them. We included them so that you can see what is possible—how you can try to make meaning for yourself out of the words of Torah.

> **Connections:** This is perhaps the most valuable part. It's a list of questions that you can ask yourself, or that others might help you think about—any of which can lead to the creation of your *devar Torah*.

Note: you don't have to like everything that's in a particular Torah portion. Some aren't that loveable. Some are hard to understand; some are about religious practices that people today might find confusing, and even offensive; some contain ideas that we might find totally outmoded.

But this doesn't have to get in the way. After all, most kids spend a lot of time thinking about stories that contain ideas that modern people would find totally bizarre. Any good medieval fantasy story falls into that category.

And we also believe that, if you spend just a little bit of time with those texts, you can begin to understand what the author was trying to say.

This volume goes one step further. Sometimes, the haftarah comes off as a second thought, and no one really thinks about it. We have tried to solve that problem by including a **summary** of each haftarah, and then a mini-sermon on the haftarah. This will help you learn how these sacred words are relevant to today's world, and even to your own life.

All Bible quotations come from the NJPS translation, which is found in the many different editions of the JPS TANAKH; in the Conservative movement's *Etz Hayim: Torah and Commentary;* in the Reform movement's *Torah: A Modern Commentary;* and in other Bible commentaries and study guides.

How Do I Write a *Devar Torah?*

It really is easier than it looks.

There are many ways of thinking about the *devar Torah.* It is, of course, a short sermon on the meaning of the Torah (and, perhaps, the haftarah) portion. It might even be helpful to think of the *devar Torah* as a "book report" on the portion itself.

The most important thing you can know about this sacred task is: *Learn* the words. *Love* the words. Teach people what it could mean to *live* the words.

Here's a basic outline for a *devar Torah:*

"My Torah portion is (name of portion)_____,
   from the book of _____, chapter

_____.

"In my Torah portion, we learn that_____
   (Summary of portion)
"For me, the most important lesson of this Torah portion is (what
   is the best thing in the portion? Take the portion as a whole;
   your *devar Torah* does not have to be only, or specifically, on the
   verses that you are reading).
"As I learned my Torah portion, I found myself wondering:
   ▸ *Raise a question that the Torah portion itself raises.*
   ▸ *"Pick a fight"* with the portion. Argue with it.
   ▸ *Answer a question* that is listed in the "Connections" section of
      each Torah portion.
   ▸ *Suggest a question to your rabbi* that you would want the rabbi
      to answer in his or her own *devar Torah* or sermon.

"I have lived the values of the Torah by _____
(here, you can talk about how the Torah portion relates to your
own life. If you have done a mitzvah project, you can talk about
that here).

How To Keep It from Being Boring
(and You from Being Bored)

Some people just don't like giving traditional speeches. From our perspective, that's really okay. Perhaps you can teach Torah in a different way—one that makes sense to you.

> Write an "open letter" to one of the characters in your Torah portion. "Dear Abraham: I hope that your trip to Canaan was not too hard . . ." "Dear Moses: Were you afraid when you got the Ten Commandments on Mount Sinai? I sure would have been . . ."
> Write a news story about what happens. Imagine yourself to be a television or news reporter. "Residents of neighboring cities were horrified yesterday as the wicked cities of Sodom and Gomorrah were burned to the ground. Some say that God was responsible . . ."
> Write an imaginary interview with a character in your Torah portion.
> Tell the story from the point of view of another character, or a minor character, in the story. For instance, tell the story of the Garden of Eden from the point of view of the serpent. Or the story of the Binding of Isaac from the point of view of the ram, which was substituted for Isaac as a sacrifice. Or perhaps the story of the sale of Joseph from the point of view of his coat, which was stripped off him and dipped in a goat's blood.
> Write a poem about your Torah portion.
> Write a song about your Torah portion.
> Write a play about your Torah portion, and have some friends act it out with you.
> Create a piece of artwork about your Torah portion.

The bottom line is: Make this a joyful experience. Yes—it could even be fun.

The Very Last Thing You Need to Know at This Point

The Torah scroll is written without vowels. Why? Don't *sofrim* (Torah scribes) know the vowels?

Of course they do.

So, why do they leave the vowels out?

One reason is that the Torah came into existence at a time when sages were still arguing about the proper vowels, and the proper pronunciation.

But here is another reason: The Torah text, as we have it today, and as it sits in the scroll, is actually *an unfinished work*. Think of it: the words are just sitting there. Because they have no vowels, it is as if they have no voice.

When we read the Torah publicly, we give voice to the ancient words. And when we find meaning in those ancient words, and we talk about those meanings, those words jump to life. They enter our lives. They make our world deeper and better.

Mazal tov to you, and your family. This is your journey toward Jewish maturity. Love it.

THE TORAH

❖ Va-yera': Genesis 18:1–22:24

Life gets interesting for Abraham and Sarah. This whole business of starting a new people and a new way of life has its difficulties. When Sarah could not have children she urged Abraham to take her slave, Hagar, and have a child with her. That child is named Ishmael. Sarah becomes pregnant at the advanced age of ninety. At that point, she cannot tolerate having Hagar and Ishmael around the camp, so she tells Abraham to kick them out.

Meanwhile, the people of the cities of Sodom and Gomorrah have become increasingly more evil. God decides to destroy the cities and their inhabitants (sounds like the Flood story, right?). Abraham argues with God and implores him to save the cities, which doesn't quite work out. Later, God tells Abraham to offer his son, Isaac, as a sacrifice. But, at the last minute Isaac is saved.

Summary

> Abraham and Sarah welcome three visitors, who announce that Sarah, age ninety, will have a child—which is really laughable—and so, Sarah laughs when she hears the news. (18:1–15)

> God and Abraham argue over the fate of the wicked cities of Sodom and Gomorrah. Abraham tries to get God to spare the cities, but his pleas are unsuccessful. (18:16–33)

> God destroys Sodom and Gomorrah. (19:1–36)

> Sarah has a child, Isaac, and at Sarah's insistence Abraham sends Hagar and Ishmael into the wilderness. (21:1–21)

> God tells Abraham to sacrifice his son Isaac, which Abraham is ready to do, but, just in the nick of time, an angel prevents the sacrifice from happening; this story is known as *Akedat Yitzchak*, "the Binding of Isaac." (22:1–19)

The Big Ideas

> **Hospitality (*hakhnasat orchim*) is an important Jewish value.**
> The Jewish people began in the desert, where welcoming
> strangers was particularly important, and that mitzvah con-
> tinues to this very day. Jews traditionally open their homes
> to guests and strangers, particularly for Shabbat and holiday
> dinners.

> **Judaism believes that it is sometimes necessary to challenge
> God.** Challenging God is an ancient tradition, and, in every gen-
> eration, that tradition appears in Jewish literature. Confronting
> God is not the same as not believing in God (you cannot confront
> something that you don't think exists). Rather, the act of con-
> fronting God affirms the close Jewish relationship with God. It
> shows that we take God seriously.

> **Evil societies destroy themselves.** While the biblical text says
> that God rained down sulfuric flames on Sodom and Gomor-
> rah, we might suggest that, in reality, those cities destroyed
> themselves through their wickedness. People and societies that
> pursue evil will eventually harm themselves. It has happened
> many times in human history—medieval Spain, Nazi Germany,
> and Communist Russia. Oppressive societies eventually simply
> fall apart.

> **Jews and Arabs are "cousin peoples."** According to tradition, the
> Arab nation is descended from Abraham's older son, Ishmael.
> Therefore, despite the painful history of Jewish-Arab relations,
> there is a deep connection between these two peoples. Hebrew
> and Arabic are "cousin" languages. So, too, there are numerous
> connections and similarities between Judaism and Islam.

> **Child sacrifice is evil.** The Canaanites and other ancient peoples
> practiced child sacrifice in their religious rituals. They believed
> that it was the way to show gratitude to God for having children,
> and to guarantee future fertility. Judaism found that practice re-
> pulsive, and it broke with that tradition. The story of the Bind-
> ing of Isaac demonstrates that God does not want children to be
> killed in God's name.

Divrei Torah

COME ON IN!

Everyone talks about Southern hospitality. No doubt about it; Southerners are very good at welcoming both friends and strangers into their homes.

That may be true, but the Jews were the original experts in hospitality.

Abraham offers hospitality to the strangers who have come to announce that Sarah will have a child. Because Abraham (along with Sarah) welcomed them with an open heart, and made sure that they were fed, he is a model for the mitzvah of hospitality (*hakhnasat orchim*).

But who are those strangers? To Abraham, they were simply *anashim*, "men" (18:2). By contrast, when Abraham's nephew, Lot, saw those same visitors in Sodom, he saw them as *malakhim*, "angels" (19:1).

In the words of a midrash: "To Abraham, endowed with great spiritual qualities, they appeared as men; but to Lot, a man poor in spiritual qualities, they appeared in the form of angels." Who wouldn't want to welcome angels to their home? For this reason, Lot's offering of hospitality to the "angels" is no big deal. But to welcome "mere" people—that is a true mitzvah.

Perhaps it is because the Jewish people started its history as a people of the desert, where resources are scarce, that they have emphasized hospitality to strangers so much. But how many of us are really that eager to open our doors, and let anyone come in and stay for a meal, or "crash" for the night? Back then it may not have been that risky (though who knows who might come visit you in the desert?). Today—it is not so safe; it can even be dangerous.

Perhaps, then, we should interpret this mitzvah of *hakhnasat orchim* differently. Many synagogues (and other houses of worship) have homeless shelters and soup kitchens where strangers are welcome. But the mitzvah of hospitality is also about how we treat newcomers in our synagogues. When "strangers" come to synagogue, do members make them feel welcome, or are they left standing around with no one to talk to? When people come to services and they are unfamiliar with the rituals and the prayer book, does someone come and help them figure out what is going on? Are our synagogues truly open to everyone—intermarried families, people with disabilities, people of different races, and LGBT people?

Rabbi Judah Loew of Prague teaches: "To welcome a guest into your home and treat him with respect because he is created in the likeness and image of God—this is considered like honoring God." So, like Abraham, when we open our homes and our synagogues—and our lives—to strangers and friends alike, maybe God is present for us and for them.

CHALLENGING GOD: A JEWISH MITZVAH

When God told Abraham that the wicked cities of Sodom and Gomorrah were about to be destroyed, Abraham argued that they should be spared. This is one of the most notable aspects of Abraham's character: he had the courage to challenge God.

The Jewish tradition does not criticize Abraham for doing so; far from it, Abraham is a hero for trying to reason with God! In the words of a midrash: "Abraham said to God: 'Master of the universe, You are in danger of causing embarrassment to Yourself. You don't want people to say that this is the way You operate. You destroyed the generation of the Flood; You destroyed the Tower of Babel. You want people to think that you're still at it?"

Judaism does not believe that we should have blind faith in God; rather, our faith should always be open to questions and challenges. When we question God, or raise challenges to our faith and our traditions, we are not being disloyal. Quite the opposite; such acts show that we are mature enough to take our relationship with God seriously.

Many people simply don't appreciate that Judaism's questioning nature is one of the best things that the religion has going for it. The other two major Western religions—Christianity and Islam—are more focused on absolute faith and true belief. People who question the divinity of Jesus Christ don't always have an easy time of it in their churches. The very word "Islam" means "to surrender one's will to God." To be a good Christian or Muslim, you need to have faith. By contrast, Judaism has always cared more about right action than right belief.

There is a long history of Jewish heroes confronting God. It started with Abraham. Then there's Moses, who challenges God when God wants to destroy the Jewish people at the incident of the Golden Calf. And, in his misery, Job cries out to God and demands to know why he is suffering so terribly. A famous talmudic sage, Elisha ben Avuya, was so upset with God that he actually said: "There is no Judge and there is no justice!" And the tradition goes all the way to Tevye in the musical *Fiddler on the Roof*—"God, I know that we are the Chosen People. But could you choose another people once in a while?"

Just as we challenge God, we must also challenge the evil that occurs in society—even when it seems that it is useless to do so. The writer Elie Wiesel tells this story: "A righteous man came to Sodom and pleaded with the people to change their ways. No one listened. Finally, he sat in the middle of the city and simply screamed. Someone asked him, 'Do you think that will change anyone?' 'No,' said the righteous man. 'But at least, they will not change me.'"

Connections

> Has anyone ever offered you hospitality? Have you ever offered someone hospitality? What did you most appreciate? What do you think your guests most appreciated? How did it make you feel?

> Does your synagogue do a good job of welcoming people? How can you help your synagogue improve how it does this?

> Do you agree that wicked societies ultimately harm themselves? What are some examples from history? Is Nazi Germany an example of this? Are there societies that have changed for the better? Would that describe what happened in the American South during the civil rights period?

> Have there been times when you have wanted to challenge God? If yes, what did you want to say? What kind of courage did that take?

> Despite the painful history that has existed between Jews and Arabs, there have been deep connections between these peoples. What have some of them been? Do those connections make peace possible? What does it mean that according to tradition the Jews and Arabs can both trace their ancestry back to Abraham?

THE HAFTARAH

❖ Va-yera': 2 Kings 4:1–37

Sometimes miracles do happen. Take the story from this week's haftarah, for example. Elisha is a prophet and a "man of God"—a wonder-worker in ancient Israel. Elisha visits a widow who is facing one of the worst situations imaginable. She has borrowed money and put her sons up as collateral for the loan. She cannot repay her debt, and the creditor is coming to take her sons. Elisha "magically" takes some of her oil and multiplies it for her, so that she can sell the oil to pay her debt.

Elisha then visits a childless woman and her elderly husband in Shunem. She offers him hospitality (actually, she builds him a room to use whenever he is in town). In gratitude for their hospitality, Elisha promises her that she will have a child—and she does. Sometime later, her child falls ill and dies, but Elisha brings the child back to life.

This story is a flashback to the Torah portion. Abraham and Sarah were too old to have children. They offer hospitality to three men, who turn out to be angels. Then, amazingly, Sarah becomes pregnant and Isaac is born. Birth is a miracle; how much more so when a couple thinks they cannot conceive a child and then do.

Seen Any Miracles Lately?

The theologian and social activist Abraham Joshua Heschel used to begin his lectures with the following words: "My friends, a great miracle happened this morning!" When people asked, "What? What was the miracle?" Heschel would answer, "The sun came up." While it may not seem like a miracle that the sun comes up every day, Rabbi Heschel was making the following point: wondrous and dramatic things happen all the time—if you choose to notice them.

But, seriously, what kinds of miracles did Elisha "really" perform? Look at the first story. It is about economic justice and injustice. The woman must leave her children with a debt collector as collateral on a loan. Elisha comes and mysteriously increases the amount of oil that she has. She sells the vessels of oil, which brings her enough money so that she can buy her children out of debt slavery. (Sounds like the famous Hanukkah miracle—the "one night of oil that lasts for eight nights" miracle—doesn't it?)

Yes, the "one vessel of oil producing many vessels of oil" bit seems like magic. But the far more interesting miracle in the story is this one: "Go, he said, and borrow vessels outside, from all your neighbors, empty vessels, as many as you can. . . . They kept bringing [vessels] to her and she kept pouring" (4:3–4). The "miracle" is that the woman was not left alone. Her community—her neighbors—helped her. They brought the vessels to her, and the vessels became filled. And why is that a sort of miracle (or at least a great blessing)? Because they could have simply decided to do nothing, but instead an entire community rallied around the woman in need.

And then, the two miracles for the woman in Shunem. Elisha promises her that she will have a child, even though her husband is very old. That certainly seems miraculous.

What about bringing the child back to life? There is a very old and powerful idea that God will, someday at the end of history, revive the dead. In the *Gevurot* prayer in the traditional Conservative and Orthodox liturgy, we find: "Your might, O Lord, is boundless. You give life to the dead; great is Your saving power." Yes, many contemporary Jews believe that God can revive the dead. But Elisha also acted—by performing an ancient form of CPR! (4:34).

As the Talmud teaches: "Don't rely on miracles." You have to make them happen.

❖ Notes

❖ Notes

Lightning Source UK Ltd.
Milton Keynes UK
UKHW041008171122
412280UK00020B/235